DANGEROUS OR ENDANGERED?

Discover the Fascinating Truths of 25 Marine Creatures!

Written by Neo Mei Lin

Illustrated by Adel Lee

WS Education

NEW JERSEY • LONDON • SINGAPORE • BEIJING • SHANGHAI • HONG KONG • TAIPEI • CHENNAI

Published by

WS Education, an imprint of
World Scientific Publishing Co. Pte. Ltd.
5 Toh Tuck Link, Singapore 596224
USA office: 27 Warren Street, Suite 401-402, Hackensack, NJ 07601
UK office: 57 Shelton Street, Covent Garden, London WC2H 9HE

National Library Board, Singapore Cataloguing in Publication Data
Name(s): Neo, Mei Lin. | Lee, Adel, illustrator.
Title: Dangerous or endangered? : discover the fascinating truths of 25 marine creatures / written by Neo Mei Lin ; illustrated by Adel Lee.
Description: Singapore : WS Education, [2025]
Identifier(s): ISBN 978-981-98-0215-9 (hardcover) | ISBN 978-981-98-0216-6 (paperback) | ISBN 978-981-98-0217-3 (ebook for institutions) | ISBN 978-981-98-0218-0 (ebook for individuals)
Subject(s): LCSH: Marine animals--Juvenile literature. | Marine biology--Juvenile literature.
Classification: DDC 591.77--dc23

British Library Cataloguing-in-Publication Data
A catalogue record for this book is available from the British Library.

Disclaimer: The views expressed are those of the author and do not necessarily reflect the views of The Pew Charitable Trusts.

Desk Editor: Daniele Lee

Printed in Malaysia

INTRODUCTION

Making up nearly 70% of the Earth's surface, the ocean is bustling with fascinating wildlife and teeming with mysteries waiting to be solved! Despite the advancements in ocean research, much of the ocean is still unexplored, making it one of the least understood places in the universe. The same can be said about the wildlife in the ocean, where our limited knowledge of marine creatures can lead to misconceptions about them.

Some marine creatures have a bad reputation because of their scary name, bizarre appearance or massive body size. But... are they really dangerous to humans, or are our actions more dangerous to them? In this book, you'll learn more about 25 incredible marine animals that could be dangerous, endangered or both!

Let's dive in to find out!

CONTENTS

DUGONG

IS IT A MERMAID?

Sailors and sea nomads across cultures believed that the dugongs were "young women of the sea" or mermaids! This belief is due to the way they rise out of the ocean gracefully with their fluke-like tails. In the island country of Palau, stories of young women transforming into dugongs to help fishermen lost at sea continue to capture people's imagination.

SCAREDY COWS

Dugongs are very shy and gentle animals. However, these curious animals may sometimes swim up to you. Though they are not known to be dangerous, when you do see dugongs in the wild, make sure to have no contact with them at all times.

RELATED TO ELEPHANTS

The dugong's closest living land relative is the elephant. And they have one thing in common – their tusks! Dugongs have erupted tusks that are only visible in adult males and very old females. The freshwater manatee is another aquatic relative of the dugong, but it does not grow tusks.

GRASS LOVERS

Cows eat grass, and dugongs eat seagrass. Their love for seagrasses has earned them the "sea cow" nickname! They can graze on these underwater plants day and night. An adult dugong is said to eat between 28 kg to 40 kg of seagrasses per day!

HELPING SEAGRASSES GROW

Protecting dugongs is good for seagrass beds, as they help disperse seagrass seeds. Dugongs will spread these seeds by eating and pooping them out as they travel long distances. This action helps seagrass to grow and colonise new sea space!

STRUCK BY A BOAT

A major threat to dugongs is fishing, as they accidentally get caught and drown in fishing nets or they get struck by boats. These threats have caused dugong numbers to decline or vanish from their habitats in some areas.

CREATURE REPORT

Common name: Dugong
Species name *gong dugon*
Type: Mammal (Class Mammalia)

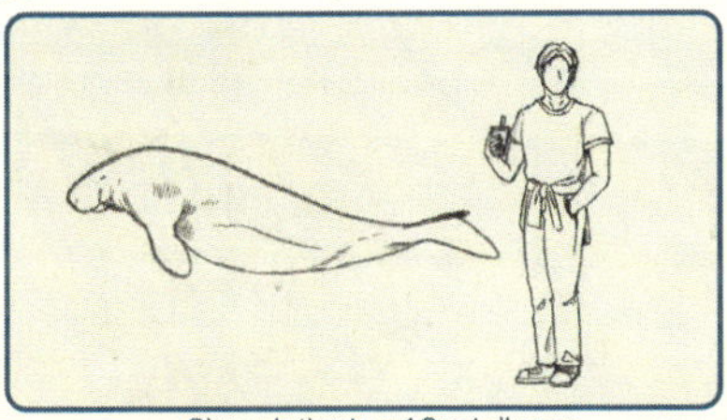

Size relative to a 1.8m tall man

Lifespan in the wild:
60-70 years

Size:
Up to 3 m long

Weight:
Up to 420 kg

DANGEROUS ✗
ENDANGERED ✓

ORCA

KILLER WHALES

Orcas are powerful apex predators, eating at the top of food webs. These “assassin whales” or *ballena asesina* in Spanish are not considered a danger to humans. Instead, they take on other larger whales, as witnessed by ancient sailors, who gave them their nickname, killer whales.

WOLVES OF THE SEA

These highly intelligent marine mammals often hunt in groups like a pack of wolves, teaming up to overpower larger prey. Orcas living in different places have varying diets. Some eat small fish like herrings, while others catch large prey such as elephant seals, blue whales and even the fearsome great white sharks!

OCEANIC DOLPHINS

Orcas are whales that have teeth. They are also the largest members of the oceanic dolphin family. With their recognisable black-and-white body colours, they can be found in every ocean. Sadly, they are threatened by habitat loss, entanglement in fishing gear and oil spills.

LIGHT SLEEPERS

Orcas take multiple naps throughout the day! This allows them to keep alert to their surroundings at all times. When they do sleep, one half of their brain shuts down to rest while the other half stays awake to control breathing and watch out for danger!

WAY OF LIFE

Like humans, orcas have their own unique cultures and vocal dialects. This knowledge is passed down from elders to the younger generations. Orca culture is said to shape behaviours such as what to eat, how to catch prey, what they do for fun and even their choice of mates!

MISSING FAMILY

Orcas were once captured and kept in captivity for aquariums. Losing family members can affect the survival of those left behind, because of the close bonds formed within pods. Until today, some orca pods who have lost their families to capture have not fully recovered their numbers.

CREATURE REPORT

Common name: Orca
Species name: *Orcinus orca*
Type: Mammal (Class Mammalia)

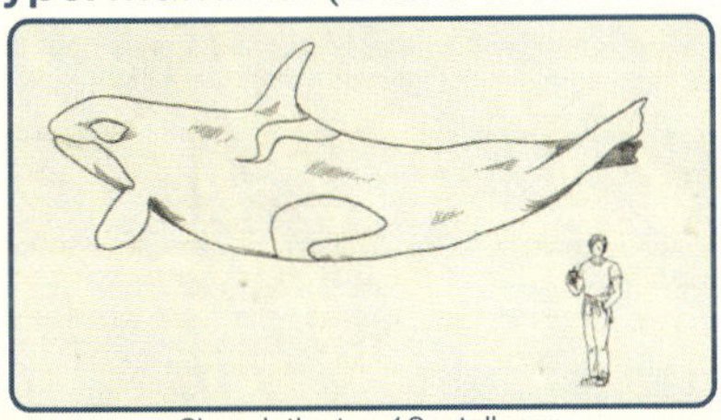

Size relative to a 1.8m tall man

Lifespan in the wild:
Up to 30-60 years for males and up to 50-90 years for females

Size:
Up to 9.8 m long

Weight:
Up to 11,000 kg

DANGEROUS ☒
ENDANGERED ☑

LEATHERBACK SEA TURTLE

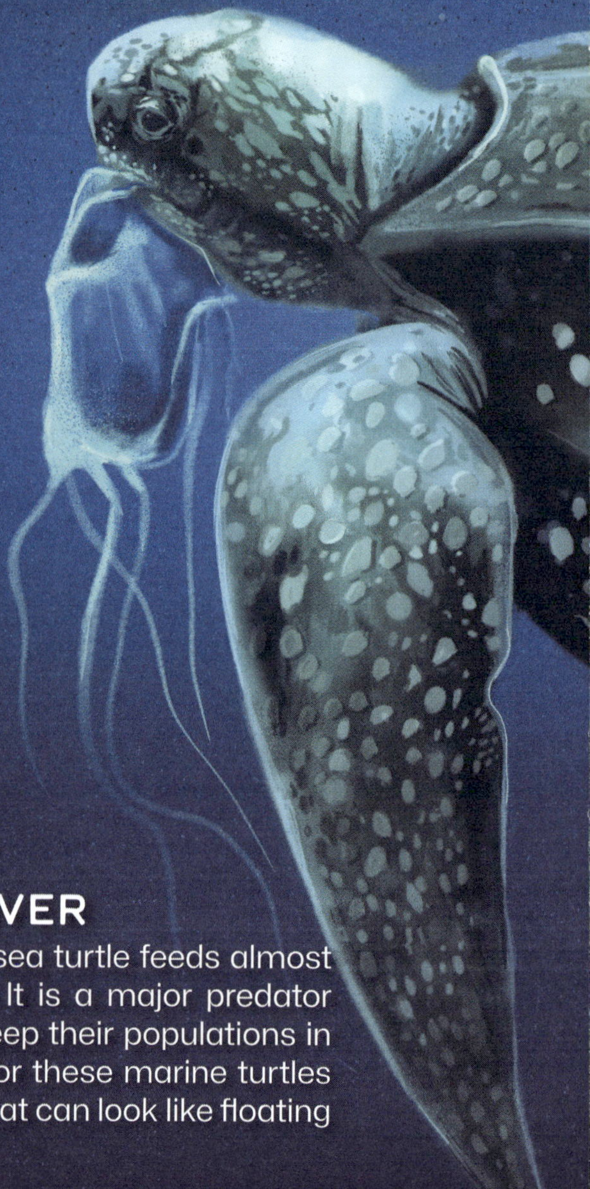

JELLYFISH LOVER

The adult leatherback sea turtle feeds almost exclusively on jellyfish. It is a major predator of jellyfish and helps keep their populations in check. A rising threat for these marine turtles is eating plastic bags that can look like floating jellyfish in the ocean.

WORLD RECORD HOLDER

Leatherback sea turtles are amazing swimmers! They are one of the deepest diving marine animals, reaching depths as great as 1,280 m. They are also the fastest-swimming reptiles, holding the record in the 1992 Guinness Book of World Records for moving at 35.28 kilometres per hour in the water!

"WALKED" WITH DINOSAURS

Of all sea turtle species, the leatherback sea turtle is the most unique of them. This old reptile is the last of its family, who has been around since the age of the dinosaurs! It is also the only species that lacks scales and a hard shell. Instead, it has a tough leathery skin.

HOT GIRLS, COOL BOYS

Unlike humans, sea turtles do not carry the genes that decide the sex of an individual. Instead, their sex is determined by the temperature of their nests. Warmer weather tends to produce more female hatchlings in the nest, while cooler temperatures produce more male hatchlings. This is also known as temperature-dependent sex determination (TSD).

PERILOUS LIFE JOURNEY

Sea turtle hatchlings have a really tough start to life! As they dig their way out of the nests, hatchlings may be eaten by birds, snakes and crabs. Even after reaching the sea, they have to watch out for sharks and big fish! Only some of them will make it to adulthood.

LIVING FOSSIL

The ancient leatherback sea turtle is highly vulnerable to extinction. It faces many dangers, including the loss of nesting habitats, illegal poaching of sea turtle eggs for food, drowning in fishing nets and climate change. We may soon lose this species that has outlived the dinosaurs.

CREATURE REPORT

Common name: Leatherback Sea Turtle
Species name: *Dermochelys coriacea*
Type: Reptile (Class Reptilia)

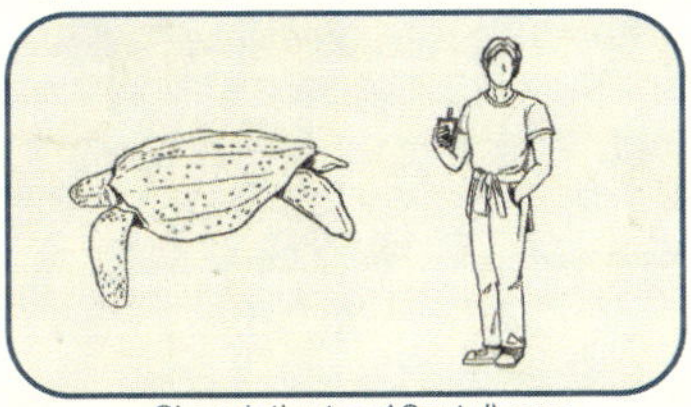

Size relative to a 1.8m tall man

Lifespan in the wild:
Up to
50 years

Size:
Up to
2 m long

Weight:
Up to 900 kg

DANGEROUS ☒
ENDANGERED ☑

BANDED SEA KRAIT

DEADLY SEA SERPENT

The banded sea krait and all other sea snakes are highly venomous! It can produce a very potent neurotoxin venom that affects the nervous system of prey. Thankfully, the banded sea krait is not aggressive and rarely poses a threat to humans unless provoked.

AMPHIBIOUS LIFESTYLE

The banded sea krait is adapted to both land and sea. When in the water, it is an excellent swimmer as it has a long, streamlined body with a flattened paddle-like tail. Unlike most sea snakes, it has large belly scales (similar to land snakes) that allow it to move around on land.

LIVING ON LAND

The banded sea krait often comes ashore to sunbathe, to shed skin, to digest food, and to mate and lay eggs. While it has lungs to fill with air during visits to the surface, this sea krait is also able to absorb oxygen into its bloodstream through the skin!

EGG-LAYING SEA SNAKE

During a single breeding season, a female banded sea krait can mate with more than one partner. The male would court and escort a female during mating for several days. After mating, the female could lay and deposit up to 10 eggs per clutch in the crevices until hatching.

MULTIPLE SPOUSES

True sea snakes usually give birth to live young. But this is not the case for the banded sea krait, which is oviparous. This means it lays eggs that will grow up outside the mother's body. Eggs of this sea krait must also remain on land because they will suffocate underwater.

LOSING HOMES

Habitat destruction and coastal development are major threats to the banded sea kraits. This may entail losing shore habitats required for digesting food and laying eggs. While the species face some threats, their population numbers appear stable worldwide.

CREATURE REPORT

Common name: Banded Sea Krait
Species name: *Laticauda colubrina*
Type: Reptile (Class Reptilia)

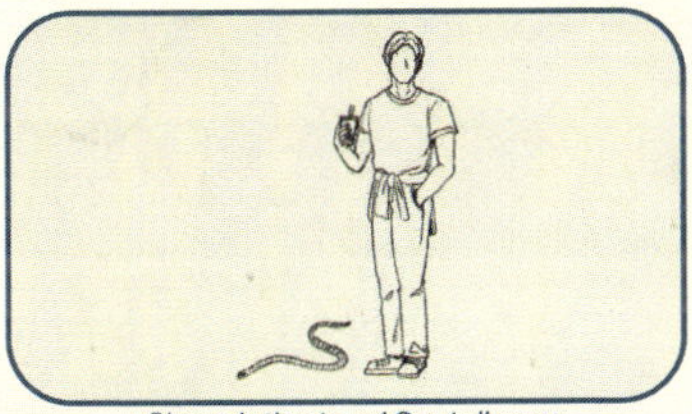

Size relative to a 1.8m tall man

Lifespan in the wild:
Around 20 years

Size:
Up to 87 cm for males and up to 142 cm for females

Weight:
0.6 to 1.8 kg

DANGEROUS ✓
ENDANGERED ✗

COOKIECUTTER SHARK

COOKIE MAKER

The cookiecutter shark got its name from making cookie-shaped wound marks! It feeds by taking a chunk of flesh from the prey's body, but these bites are non-fatal. Its teeth are also the largest compared to its body size of any known shark!

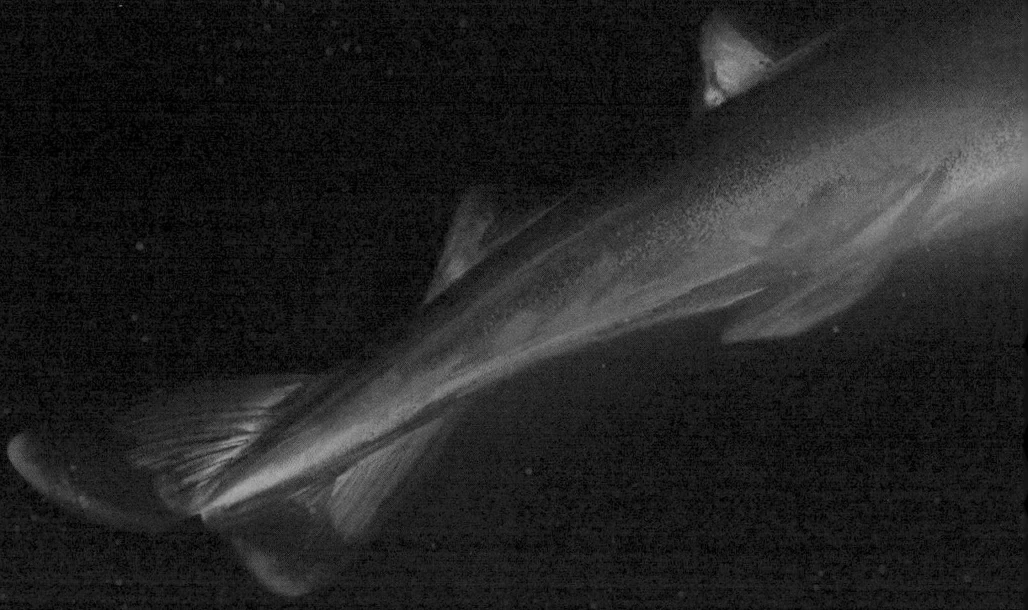

GLOW IN THE DARK

The cookiecutter shark gives off a vivid greenish glow in the dark because it has light-emitting organs in its skin called photophores. The glow (or bioluminescence) continues even after the shark has been taken out of the water.

DISGUISE IN GLOW

The green bioluminescence can help this deep-sea shark to camouflage. Known as counterillumination, an animal below the cookiecutter shark cannot see it very well because the light emitted blends the shark well with the environment.

NIGHTLY MIGRATION

A cookiecutter shark prefers to stay in the deep waters – as deep as 3,500 m! It can also vertically migrate to the surface at night for feeding before going back down below 1,000 m during the day.

MUNCHING ON THE WRONG FOOD?

Cookiecutter sharks are not very good at recognising their food. They often damage submarine cables, mistaking them for blubber. In very rare cases, they have bitten people who swim at night. Luckily, their bites are non-fatal!

CAUGHT IN THE NET

Although the cookiecutter sharks are not a target for fishery, they occasionally get caught in trawl nets and longlines. Scientists do not think they are in danger now because they are widely distributed with low capture rates.

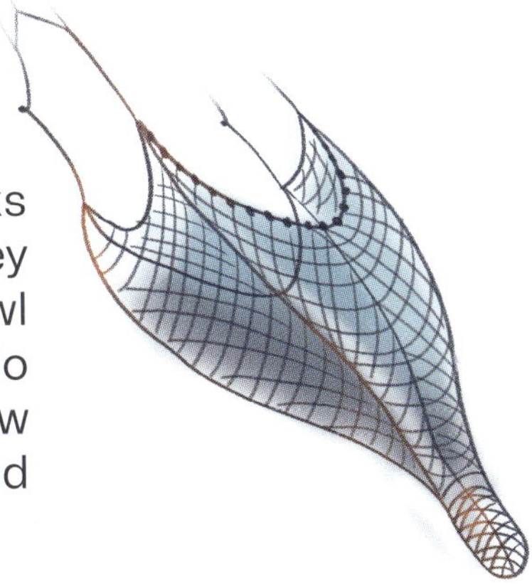

CREATURE REPORT

Common name: Cookiecutter Shark
Species name: *Isistius brasiliensis*
Type: Fish (Class Chondrichthyes)

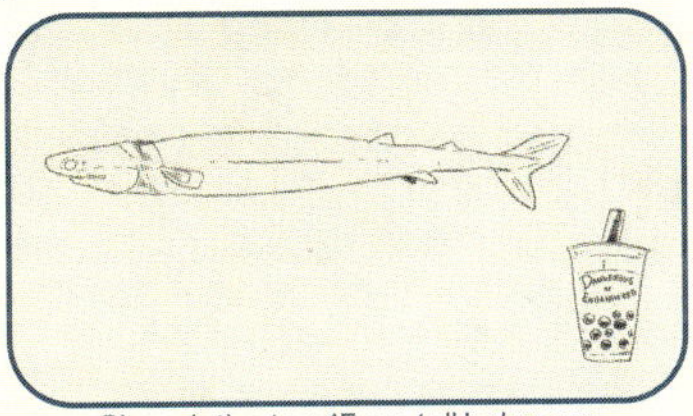

Size relative to a 15 cm tall boba cup

Lifespan in the wild:
Estimated to be around 25 years

Size:
Up to 42 cm for males and up to 56 cm for females

Weight:
220 to 280 g

DANGEROUS ☒

ENDANGERED ☒

COFFIN RAY

NOTHING LIKE A COFFIN

The coffin ray is nothing like its namesake – the coffin box. Instead, it has an almost featureless pear-shaped body and a very stumpy tail. This endemic species lives in the nearshore coastal waters of Australia at no deeper than 80 m.

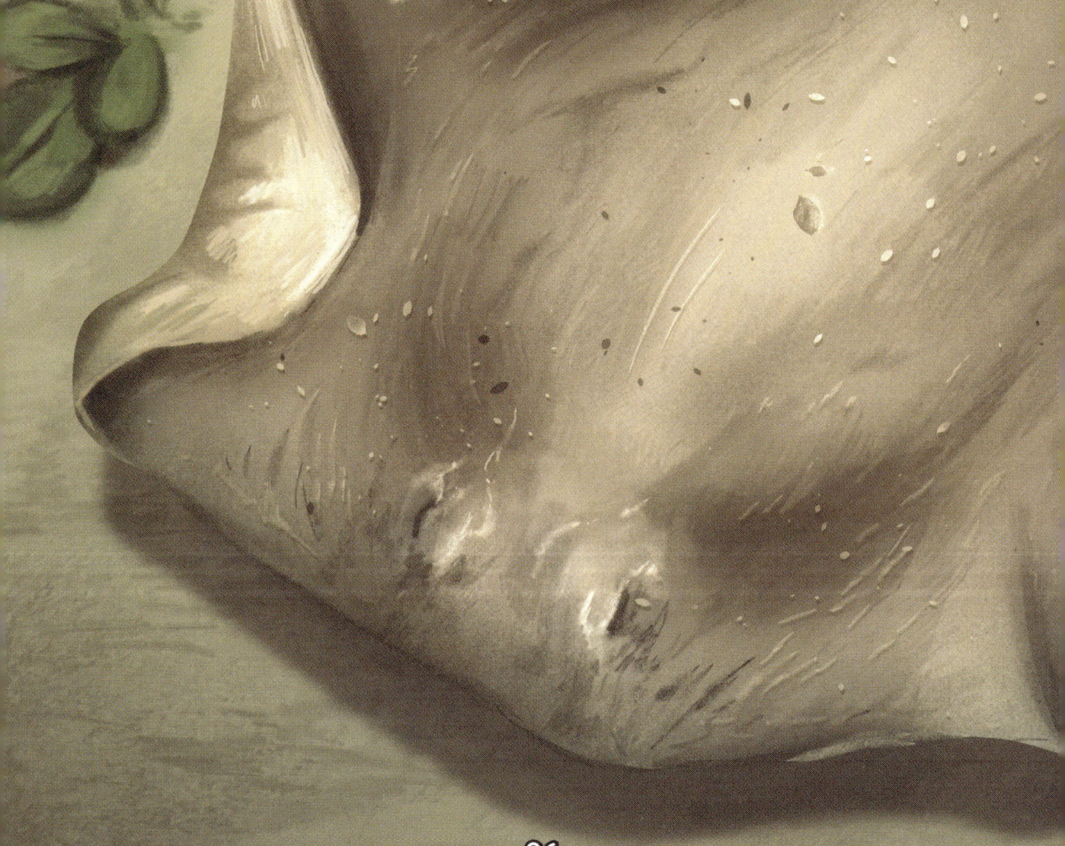

STUNNED PREY

A coffin ray can deliver strong electric shocks of up to 200 volts of electricity! The electric organ in each pectoral fin consists of muscle tissues forming a vertical stack of jelly-filled "electric plates" that work like a battery. It uses electricity to shock its prey and warn off predators.

BITING MORE THAN IT CAN CHEW

The typical diet of a coffin ray is made up of crabs, worms and fish. Occasionally, this ambush predator may tackle and feed on very large fishes exceeding its body size. Amazingly, remains of penguins and rats have also been found in the stomachs of coffin rays!

NURSING BABIES

A coffin ray gives birth to live babies, where they develop inside the mother's body until they are born. The growing babies first feed on the yolk early in their development. Once the yolk is eaten up, the mother's uterus makes histotroph (or "uterine milk") that sustains the babies before birth.

FEELING NUMBED

Many unsuspecting swimmers and divers have found themselves being accidentally electrocuted by the coffin ray. The shock can feel quite severe, numbing the contact area for several minutes or knocking a standing adult off his feet. Luckily, none of these effects are life-threatening.

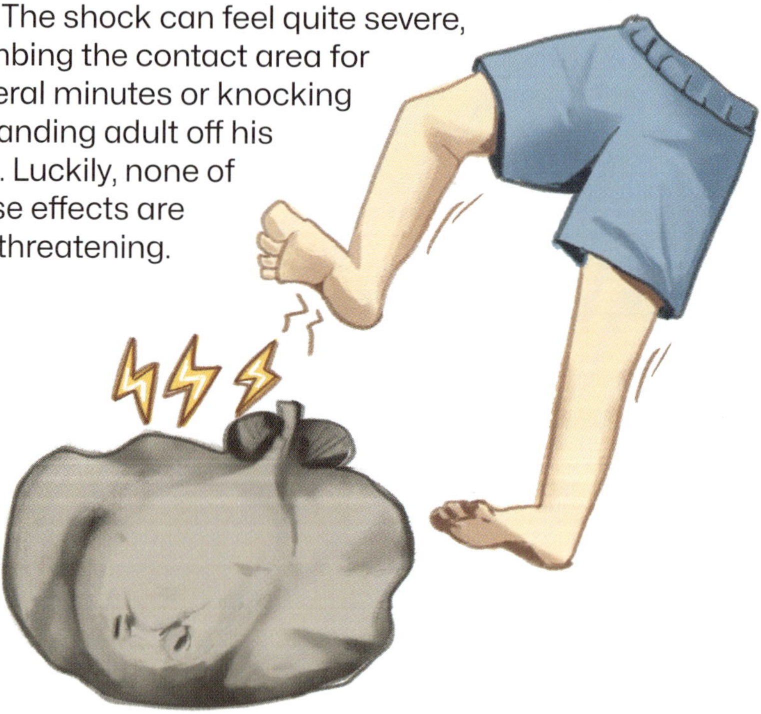

A TOUGH RAY

Coffin rays are very hardy animals that can tolerate handling and survive without water for hours. As they are not commercially valuable seafood, they are usually unharmed and fishers released them back into the water with high survival rates. There appears to be no immediate threats to this species' populations.

CREATURE REPORT

Common name: Coffin Ray
Species name: *Hypnos monopterygius*
Type: Fish (Class Chondrichthyes)

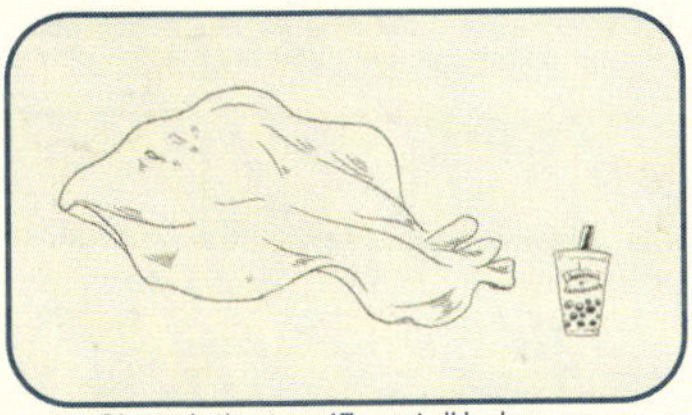

Size relative to a 15 cm tall boba cup

Lifespan in the wild:
16 to 24 years

Size:
41 to 71 cm

Weight:
6 to 13 kg

DANGEROUS ✓

ENDANGERED ✗

WHALE SHARK

I'M NOT A WHALE

The whale shark is the world's largest fish! Almost the size of a school bus, this enormous shark cruises slowly near the ocean's surface to filter feed. It opens its mouth wide, like a giant net catching anything that comes their way – mostly small fishes, fish eggs and plankton.

BONELESS FISH

Whale sharks do not have bones, as with all other sharks. Their skeletons are made of cartilage – the same tissue as human ears and nose! Cartilage is a firm but softer and more flexible tissue than bone, so it helps sharks use less energy to swim fast.

SPIKY CONTACT LENSES!

A whale shark's eyeball has over 3,000 dermal denticles! These structures are more similar to teeth than fish scales. As this unique eye protection has only been found in the whale sharks, it seems they need good vision to perceive their environment.

GENTLE GIANTS

Whale sharks are not known to be aggressive to humans despite being one of the biggest creatures in the ocean. That being said, scientists have observed that these sharks swim in the opposite direction when irresponsible tourists come too close to them!

STARRY BACKS

The patterns of spots and stripes resembling stars on every whale shark are unique to them, like your fingerprints. Scientists use these patterns to tell the giant fishes apart from each other. It also helps scientists track their migratory routes and learn more about their breeding and feeding habits.

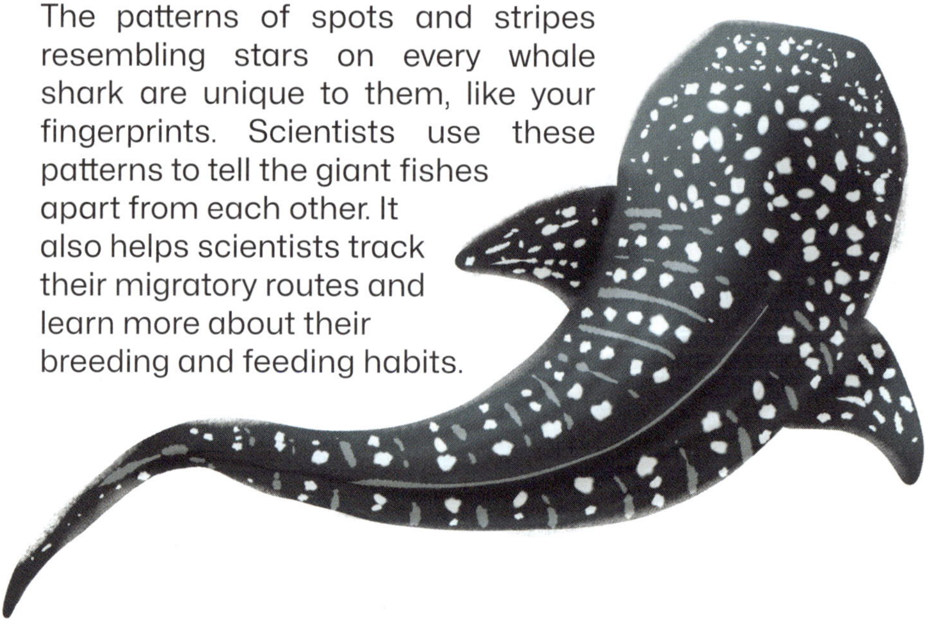

DEATH BY FISHING

Whale sharks are in danger due to many threats, including illegal fishing practices, bycatch in fishing gear, vessel strikes and oil pollution. Their populations have been declining over the years and scientists recognise the species as endangered.

CREATURE REPORT

Common name: Whale Shark
Species name: *Rhincodon typus*
Type: Fish (Class Chondrichthyes)

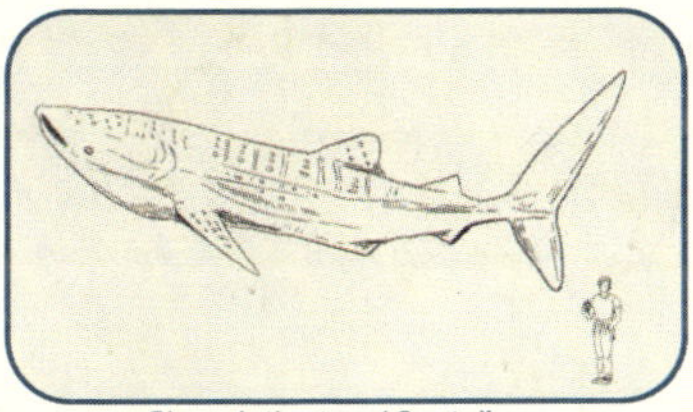

Size relative to a 1.8m tall man

Lifespan in the wild: Around 80 years

Size: Up to 8-9 m for males and up to 15 m for females

Weight: 20,600 kg

DANGEROUS ☒
ENDANGERED ✓

GIANT OARFISH

ROW, ROW, ROW YOUR BODY

With an oar in its name, the giant oarfish is believed to swim by "rowing" its long pelvic fins on the underside of its body. However, this is untrue. Scientists deduced that these strange pelvic fins are more likely for perceiving taste instead of moving.

SCALELESS BONY FISH

A giant oarfish lacks fish scales, which is unlike many other bony fishes. Their long, flat and tapering body has tiny hard knobs called tubercles and is covered with a silvery protective coat of guanine. It is also recognisable by the bright red crest sitting atop its large head.

TOOTHLESS SEA DRAGON

With a long snake-like body, a giant oarfish reminds you of the mythical and fearsome sea dragon. Instead of destroying ships in the open sea, the giant oarfish is rather harmless. It has a very small mouth with no teeth and feeds by capturing food with its mouth open when swimming.

THE DOOMSDAY FISH

Folktales believe that the giant oarfish is a bearer of bad news. When an oarfish is seen, it is a warning sign from higher powers that disasters such as earthquakes are about to happen. Believe it or not, 20 oarfish washed ashore just before Japan's most catastrophic earthquake in 2011!

GELATINOUS GOO

You would not find the giant oarfish on any seafood menu as it is very unappetising. People have tried eating it, but the flabby meat looks and tastes like gelatinous goo! As it is unsuitable for eating, the giant oarfish does not have any commercial value.

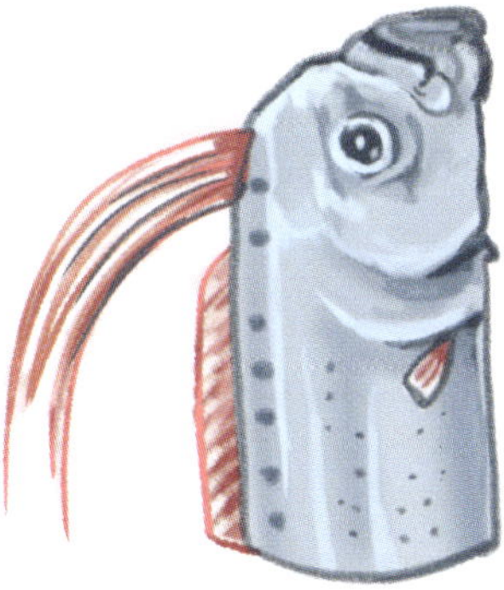

THE HARMLESS BEANPOLE

The giant oarfish is the world's longest bony fish that lives quietly in great depths of 1,000 m of temperate and tropical seas. The few people who have seen it alive in the wild remarked on its docile and curious nature – not quite your dangerous sea dragon!

CREATURE REPORT

Common name: Giant Oarfish
Species name: *Regalecus glesne*
Type: Fish (Class Actinopterygii)

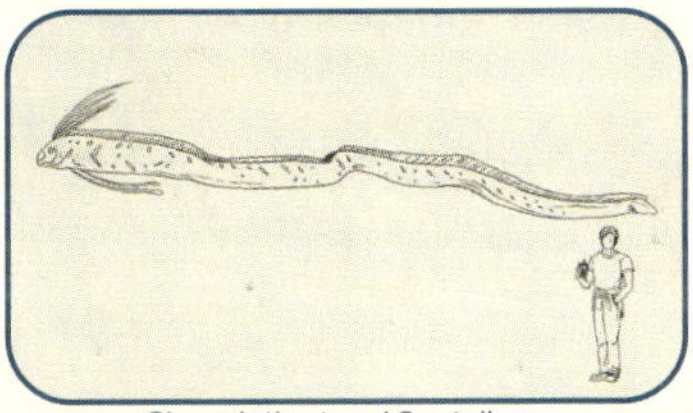

Size relative to a 1.8m tall man

Lifespan in the wild:
Unknown

Size:
11 to 17 m long

Weight:
Up to 272 kg

DANGEROUS ☒
ENDANGERED ☒

CONVICT BLENNY

FISHY FELONY?

With body colours similar to convict suits, convict blennies look like prisoners! The adult fish have black bodies with pale yellow stripes, while young fish have white stripes. These body colours are thought to protect them from predators. Contrary to their name, the convict blennies are also not related to true blennies!

MAJOR DIGGER

An adult convict blenny is an efficient tunnel engineer! It can dig, build and maintain a complex maze of burrows up to 6 m long. Seeing one in action can be tough because this highly secretive fish rarely appears outside the burrow.

BEST HOUSEKEEPER

During the day, the adult is busy "cleaning" the burrow. To upkeep its living spaces, the adult convict blenny continuously clears out mouthfuls of sand, coral rubble and other debris that can amount to up to 3 kg daily!

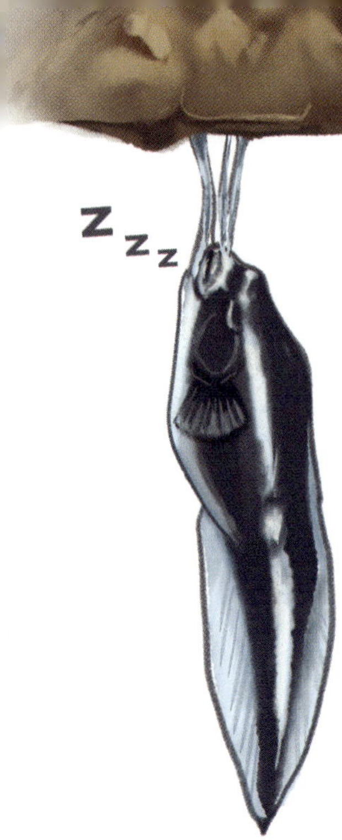

HANGING ON A THREAD

Young convict blennies have an unusual sleeping habit. Throughout the night, they hang vertically from the roofs in their burrows using thin threads of mucus coming out from their mouths!

BRINGING BACK LUNCH

The young convict blennies leave their burrow daily to search for plankton as far as 45 m away from home. When they look for food, the shoal of young fish looks like the venomous striped eel catfish! Upon return to their burrow, they would feed regurgitated plankton and mucus to the hungry adult.

AQUARIUM PETS

The convict blenny is a popular species often sold in the aquarium trade. For now, it is uncertain if the collection for the aquarium trade have impacted the wild populations, but populations of the convict blenny may not yet be threatened.

CREATURE REPORT

Common name: Convict Blenny
Species name: *Pholidichthys leucotaenia*
Type: Fish (Class Actinopterygii)

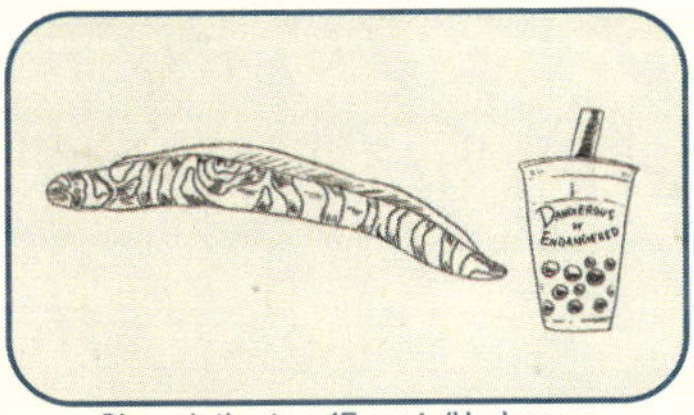

Size relative to a 15 cm tall boba cup

Lifespan in the wild:
Unknown

Size:
Up to
35 cm long

Weight:
Around 1-2 kg

DANGEROUS [X]
ENDANGERED [?]

OCEAN SUNFISH

A FLOATING HEAD?

When you see an ocean sunfish, it may look like a head swimming in mid-water! Unlike other fishes, the sunfish has an unusual appearance with a round body and short tail fin. It swims by using its long dorsal and anal fins to paddle concurrently to move forward.

BASKING IN THE SUN

The ocean sunfish can often be seen on their sides sunning themselves at the sea surface. This basking behaviour is believed to help these fish warm themselves after foraging in the deeper, colder waters. While basking, their tall dorsal fins sticking out of the water could easily be mistaken for sharks!

BURDENED WITH PARASITES

More than 40 species of parasites are known to take shelter on the ocean sunfish! That is why these fish often visit cleaning stations where cleaner wrasses and other small fish can pick at them. Breaching out of the ocean's surface is also thought to rid parasites.

BIRD MOUTH

The odd-looking ocean sunfish has a small mouth that looks like a bird's beak! This beak-like mouth is made from fused teeth plates and is always open. It feeds by sucking its food in and out repeatedly, which helps to tear the food into smaller chunks.

THE CURIOUS FISH

If you ever find yourself face to face with the ocean sunfish, do not be surprised if it comes to check you out! This fish is not known to be aggressive to humans. Instead, it approaches and investigates divers and snorkellers out of curiosity.

DEFENCELESS AGAINST MAN

While fully-grown ocean sunfish have few natural predators, they are highly vulnerable to fishing activities. Their numbers are declining because of unregulated fishing and bycatch in gillnets. Plastic bags are also especially bad because they look like their favourite food, the jellyfish.

CREATURE REPORT

Common name: Ocean Sunfish
Species name: *Mola mola*
Type: Fish (Class Actinopterygii)

Size relative to a 1.8m tall man

Lifespan in the wild:
Unknown

Size:
Up to 4 m long

Weight:
Up to 2,500 kg

DANGEROUS ☒

ENDANGERED ☑

TIGER TAIL SEAHORSE

NOT YOUR TYPICAL FISH

Instead of fish scales, the tiger tail seahorse has a thin skin covering over a set of bony plates. The latter makes it distasteful to most predators as it is too bony to eat! With no teeth and no true stomach, the food eaten goes through its digestive tube so quickly that a seahorse has to eat all day to live and grow!

DANCE PARTNERS

During courtship, the tiger tail seahorse couples come together every morning to dance! To kick-start their mating process, the male and female seahorses intertwine their prehensile tails and swim together. This dance can last up to days before the female deposits her eggs in the male's pouch.

PREGNANT DADDY

All seahorses, including the tiger tail seahorse, perform true male pregnancy. Like human moms, the male seahorse fertilises the eggs and continues to carry and grow them inside his pouch. Once they are fully grown, the male seahorse releases up to hundreds of babies at a time!

CLICK AND GROWL

A tiger tail seahorse usually makes clicking sounds to communicate in different situations, such as courting, mating and feeding. It apparently can also make a growling sound when stressed or a purring sound in a happy state. These different vocalisations could help seahorses better understand each other.

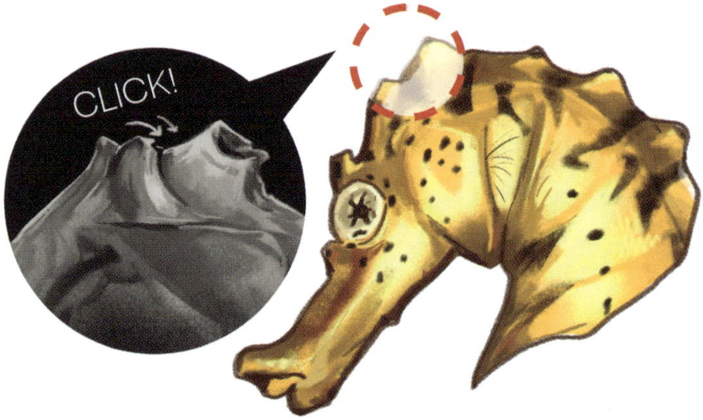

THE AQUATIC CHAMELEON

Seahorses and chameleons are surprisingly very alike! These masters of camouflage can blend in with their surroundings, which help them avoid predators and become skilful ambush predators.

They also share traits like their prehensile tails capable of grasping and eyes that move separately from each other and in all directions!

DRYING OUT

Tiger tail seahorses are threatened due to the international wildlife trade. Despite trade bans, millions of seahorses are still collected and dried for traditional medicines and as curios. These docile animals are also traded in the live ornamental trade as aquarium pets.

CREATURE REPORT

Common name: Tiger Tail Seahorse
Species name: *Hippocampus comes*
Type: Fish (Class Actinopterygii)

Size relative to a 15 cm tall boba cup

Lifespan in the wild:
3 to 5 years

Size:
Up to 18.7 cm long

Weight:
About 200 g

DANGEROUS ✗

ENDANGERED ✓

MIMIC OCTOPUS

THE ELUSIVE OCTOPUS

The mimic octopus is a native of the Indian and Pacific Oceans. It was first discovered in 1998 off the coast of Sulawesi in Indonesia. Like other octopus species, the mimic octopus can avoid detection by changing its skin colour and blending into the environment.

TRICKSTERS

A mimic octopus is capable of imitating venomous and toxic animals such as the lionfish, sea snakes and sole fish! Apart from changing its skin colour and texture, it mimics these animals by waving its arms as well. Scientists think that these forms of mimicry protect the mimic octopus from predators.

TWIST AND BEND

Without a rigid skeleton, the mimic octopus can easily twist and bend its body into various poses, just like a contortionist! The beak inside its mouth is the only hard part of the animal's body. This explains why it can escape easily by squeezing its body into tight spaces.

MUCKING AROUND

Unlike other octopuses that are nocturnal and like to hide in crevices and burrows during the day, the mimic octopus spends its day in the shallow murky areas. Because of its behavioural mimicry, it can live in open habitats with no need for hiding.

NINE BRAINS, THREE HEARTS AND BLUE BLOOD

These incredible octopuses have nine brains that control the central body and arms independently. They also have three hearts to circulate oxygenated blood around the body and gills. Unlike our red iron-based haemoglobin, the octopuses' blue blood contain copper-based haemocyanin, which are efficient at transporting oxygen for life in the sea.

HIDE AND SEEK

We know little about its lifestyle and habits because the reclusive mimic octopus hides so well. It is unlikely considered endangered for now. Unlike some other octopuses, this shy species is not poisonous. Regardless, we should still avoid touching it with our bare hands.

CREATURE REPORT

Common name: Mimic Octopus
Species name: *Thaumoctopus mimicus*
Type: Invertebrate (Class Cephalopoda)

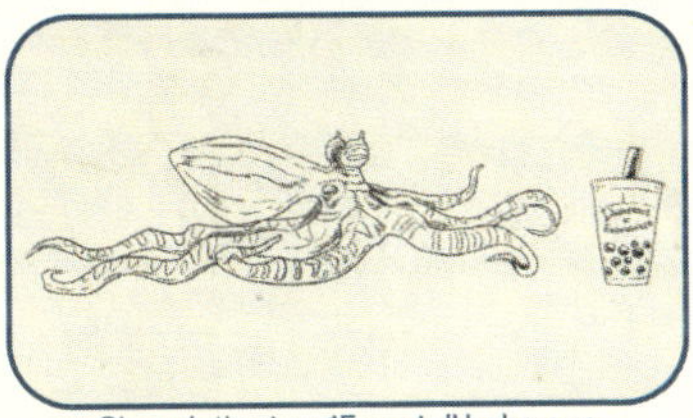

Size relative to a 15 cm tall boba cup

Lifespan in the wild:
0.75 to 2 years

Size:
60 to 70 cm

Weight:
2.3 to 9.1 kg

DANGEROUS ☒

ENDANGERED ☒

VAMPIRE SQUID

IMPOSTER SQUID

Ironically, the vampire squid is neither a squid nor an octopus! Scientists think that this species is unlike other cephalopods because of its unique features, such as the webbing between its arms, two long sensory tentacles, a pair of fins on the head and not producing any ink.

SCARE GLOW

To protect against predation, the vampire squid dazzles and confuses predators with its glowing arms. The tip of each arm contains light-producing organs known as photophores. Each arm can glow for about 10 minutes, giving the animal enough time to get away!

A VAMPIRE'S CLOAK

The vampire squid is nothing like the scary, blood-sucking vampire in myths. The namesake likely describes the dark-coloured webbing to cloak itself. When threatened, it takes on a "pineapple pose" by pulling its glowing webbed arms over the body revealing the rows of spikes to ward off predators.

GARBAGE-EATER

The vampire squid survives by feeding on the raining "rubbish" (made of dead and decaying organisms) that falls from the sea surface. It uses two long and thin tentacles to trap particles into mucus food balls before eating them. It is the only living species of cephalopod that does not eat live prey.

THE SHADOW ZONE

The vampire squid lives in the oxygen minimum zone, where the oxygen levels in the ocean are at its lowest. To survive in such a zone in the deep ocean, the vampire squid has a very slow metabolic rate that allows it to use very little oxygen. This also means that the energy from food can last longer.

DIFFICULT STUDY SUBJECT

Very little is known of the vampire squid because it is difficult for us to observe it alive as it lives at very deep depths. While it does not appear to be endangered now, it may become threatened by ocean warming and decreasing oxygen in the near future.

CREATURE REPORT

Common name: Vampire Squid
Species name: *Vampyroteuthis infernalis*
Type: Invertebrate (Class Cephalopoda)

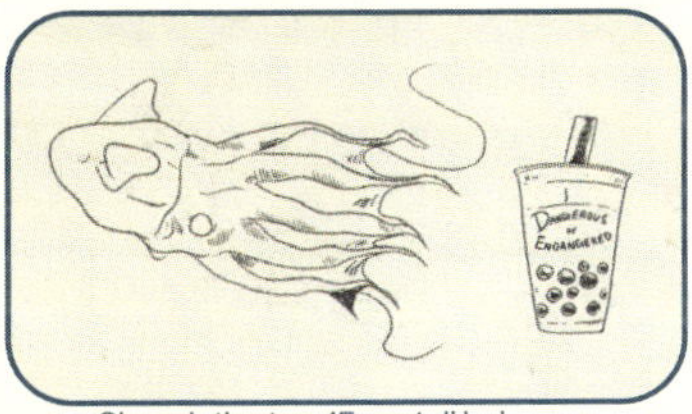

Size relative to a 15 cm tall boba cup

Lifespan in the wild:
Around
8 years

Size:
30 cm

Weight:
450 g

DANGEROUS ☒

ENDANGERED ☒

TRUE GIANT CLAM

AN OCEAN'S WONDER

The true giant clam is enormous among marine molluscs! The biggest clam was known to be 1.37 m long, while the heaviest known individual was nearly 300 kg. The latter giant clam weighs nearly as much as three newborn elephants!

MAN-EATING CLAM?

At first glance, a giant clam can look like a giant mouth with colourful fleshy lips peeking out of the shell. No wonder people thought of it as a man-eating legend capable of swallowing unsuspecting visitors in its "jaws"! But this legend is unfounded because no actual deaths have been reported.

CLAMMING UP

True giant clams can close up their shell quickly when they feel threatened. But they cannot shut their shell completely because of their fleshy tissues, which gives opponents time to react and escape. That said, it is prudent to keep your hands away from their wavy shells!

A NIGHT IN THE OCEAN

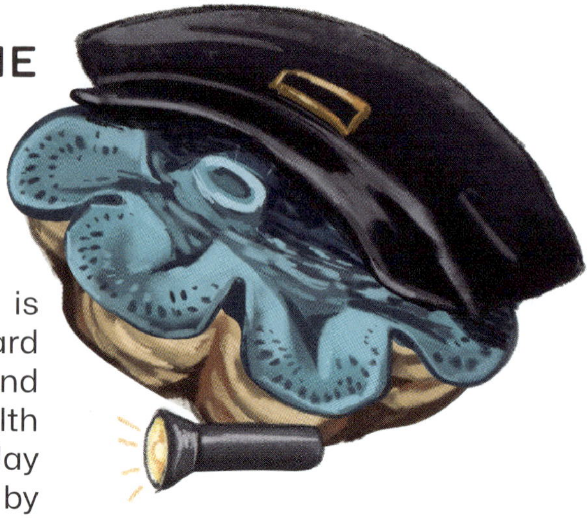

A true giant clam is like a security guard that "keeps watch" and monitors the health of coral reefs all day and night. It does so by recording and storing information about the reef's health in its shell. Scientists can later study this information by looking at the shell growth bands!

THE REEF ENGINEER

Not many marine animals can claim this title, and the true giant clam is one of them. Each giant clam is a reef builder, food factory, water filter and shelter for small marine animals, all rolled into one animal!

CANARY IN THE COAL MINE

The true giant clam is much like the canary in the coal mine for the health of coral reefs. Its rapid disappearance due to overfishing, habitat loss and climate change can also serve as early indicators of the potential threats to coral reefs.

CREATURE REPORT

Common name: True Giant Clam
Species name: *Tridacna gigas*
Type: Invertebrate (Class Bivalvia)

Size relative to a 1.8m tall man

Lifespan in the wild:
Around
50-60 years

Size:
Up to 1.3 m long

Weight:
Up to 500 kg

DANGEROUS ☒
ENDANGERED ☑

ELECTRIC FLAME SCALLOP

DISCO FLASHING

Only one bivalve in the world can make a flashing light display – the electric flame scallop. While bioluminescent organisms produce and emit light, this clam achieves a shimmering display by reflecting light off its highly reflective silica-rich cells found in its tissues.

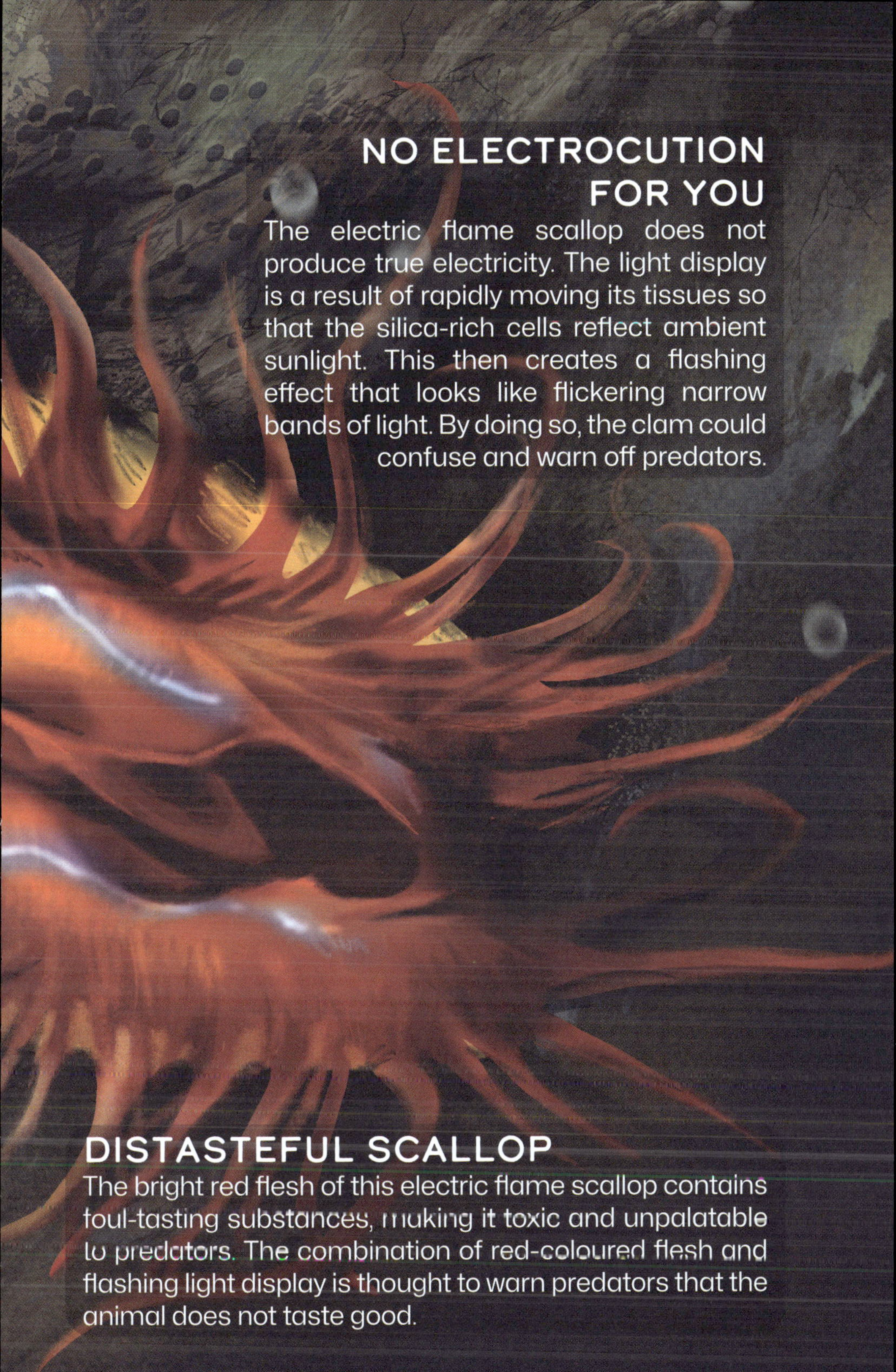

NO ELECTROCUTION FOR YOU

The electric flame scallop does not produce true electricity. The light display is a result of rapidly moving its tissues so that the silica-rich cells reflect ambient sunlight. This then creates a flashing effect that looks like flickering narrow bands of light. By doing so, the clam could confuse and warn off predators.

DISTASTEFUL SCALLOP

The bright red flesh of this electric flame scallop contains foul-tasting substances, making it toxic and unpalatable to predators. The combination of red-coloured flesh and flashing light display is thought to warn predators that the animal does not taste good.

ACIDIC SPIT!

To be the most unappealing prey, the electric flame scallop also spits acidic mucus at its predators! Scientists observed that this clam sprayed an awful-tasting sulphuric acid at a mantis shrimp. The mixture immobilises the predator, making it unresponsive for 15 minutes!

PHYTOPLANKTON CONNOISSEUR

Like other clams, the electric flame scallop mainly feeds on phytoplankton (or microscopic marine algae cells) in the water. It filters water through its mouth opening and gills, then captures phytoplankton particles in its sticky mucus.

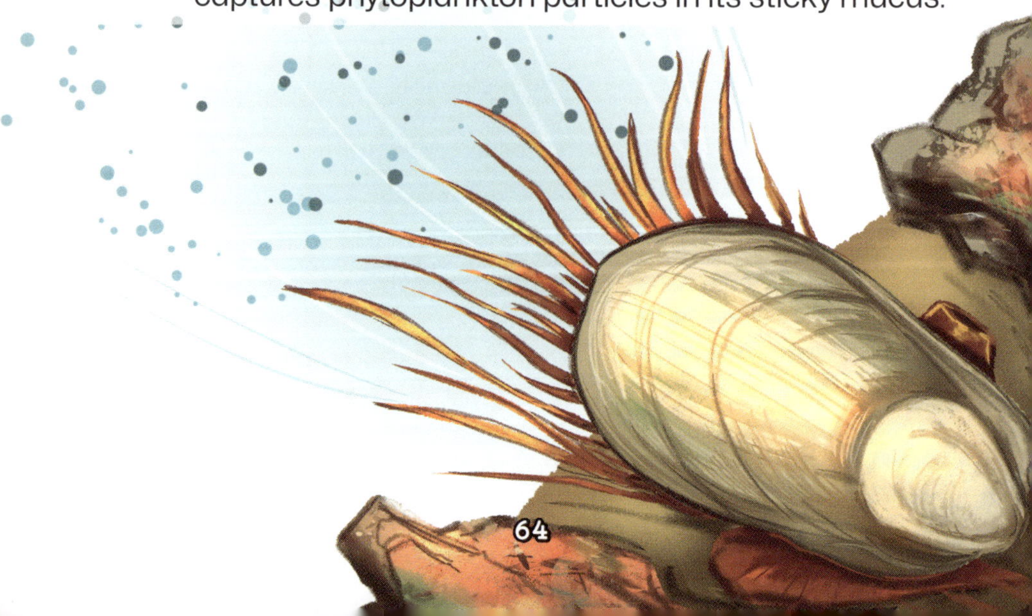

LESS FOOD, FEWER BABIES

Phytoplankton is an important ingredient that helps these clams reproduce and thrive successfully. However, the rising ocean temperatures are predicted to negatively impact phytoplankton growth. Having less phytoplankton can spell trouble for their populations in the future.

CREATURE REPORT

Common name: Electric Flame Scallop
Species name: *Ctenoides ales*
Type: Invertebrate (Class Bivalvia)

Size relative to a 15 cm tall boba cup

Lifespan in the wild:
Estimated up to 30 years

Size:
Up to 8 cm long

Weight:
Unknown

DANGEROUS ☒
ENDANGERED ?

MAGICIAN'S CONE SNAIL

DEADLY TASERS

Cone snails are dangerous beauties. Under their pretty ornate shells, they produce a lethal dose of complex venom. The venom contains great amounts of toxins known as conotoxins. Like all cone snails, a single sting from the magician's cone snail spells instant death for its prey.

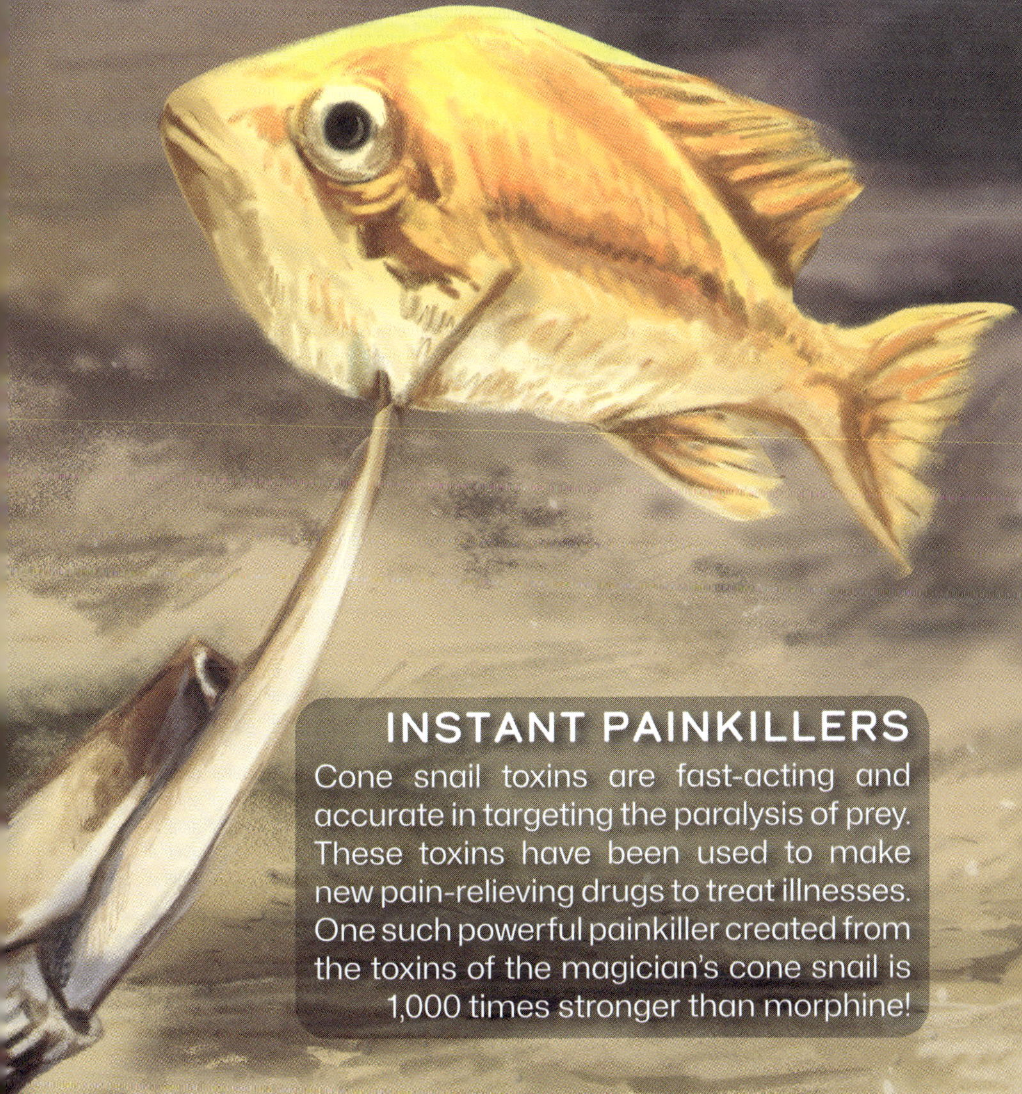

INSTANT PAINKILLERS

Cone snail toxins are fast-acting and accurate in targeting the paralysis of prey. These toxins have been used to make new pain-relieving drugs to treat illnesses. One such powerful painkiller created from the toxins of the magician's cone snail is 1,000 times stronger than morphine!

SPECIALISED HUNTERS

The adult magician's cone snail "goes fishing" with its tubular mouthpart, which lures a fish closer. It then injects venom with its harpoon-like teeth before reeling in its prey to feed. The juvenile of this cone snail prefers to stab and stalk worms instead.

PRETTY-LOOKING SHELLS

For centuries, shell collectors around the world seek out beautiful and rare seashells such as those of the cone snails. These snails, including the magician's cone snail, produce beautifully patterned and colourful shells. Their perfect geometric conical shapes also make them highly desirable.

CIGARETTE SNAIL

Looking nothing like a cigarette, this nickname given to the magician's cone snail and their relatives jokingly reflects their speed of killing. It is said that a stung person would probably only have time to smoke one cigarette before dying!

MOVE AWAY!

Despite their terrifying reputations, cone snails are not aggressive by nature. However, they are all highly venomous and capable of stinging humans. So if you ever see a marine snail with a cone-shaped shell in the wild, never, ever touch it!

CREATURE REPORT

Common name: Magician's Cone Snail
Species name: *Conus magus*
Type: Invertebrate (Class Gastropoda)

Size relative to a 15 cm tall boba cup

Lifespan in the wild:
10 to 20 years

Size:
16 to 94 mm

Weight:
Around 100 g

DANGEROUS ✓
ENDANGERED ✗

TIGER COWRIE

WHERE IS THE TIGER?

Unlike its common name, a tiger cowrie looks nothing like the land mammal. The highly ornamented seashell is spotted and not striped. Interestingly, the young tiger cowries have colour patterns resembling tiger stripes, which could explain the common name.

SHINY SHELLS

The tiger cowrie moves its fleshy tissue around the shell to keep it clean and polished – just like a wiper! This self-polishing behaviour also prevents other small organisms from damaging the shell surface.

PROTECTIVE MOTHERS

The female tiger cowrie displays a unique parental care behaviour unlike any other marine sea snails. After mating with a male, the female cowrie lays her pinkish-purple eggs and sits over them by covering them with her foot. She will protect her eggs until the babies are ready to hatch!

GOOD LUCK CHARMS

People believe that cowrie shells can bring them good luck and prosperity. For example, the tiger cowrie shell is worn or carried around to repel negative energies, ward off evil and protect against physical harm.

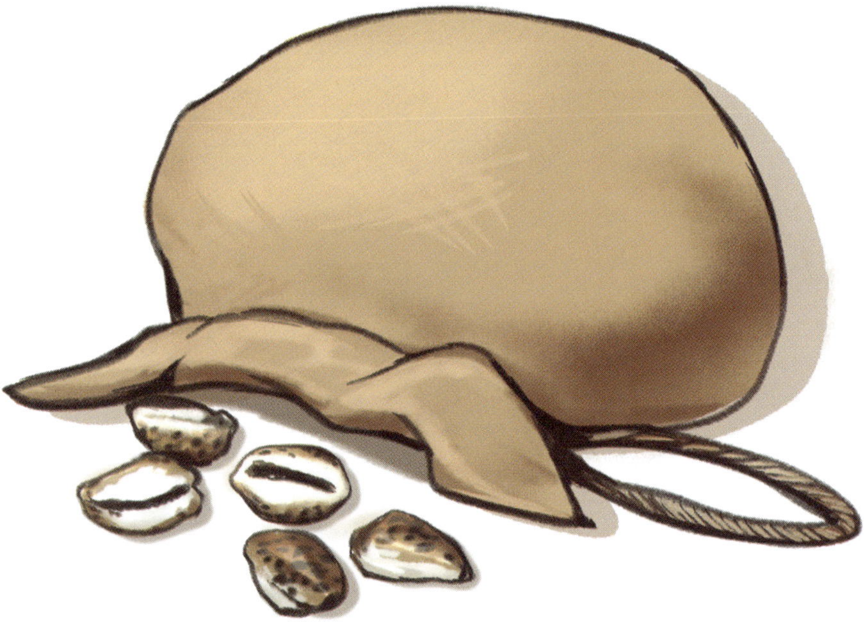

SHELL MONEY

One of the most successful forms of money was the cowrie shells. They were widely used to trade goods and services throughout Africa, Asia, Europe and Oceania. Why? Well, because the shells are easy to recognise, light to carry and easy to count. Most importantly, cowrie shells are difficult to fake!

SUFFERING FOR SOUVENIRS

Sadly, the curio trade is over-collecting vulnerable species like the tiger cowrie. Because cowrie shells are colourful and beautiful to look at, people collect them as keepsakes or for jewellery. Live cowries are also taken from the wild for the aquarium trade.

CREATURE REPORT

Common name: Tiger Cowrie
Species name: *Cypraea tigris*
Type: Invertebrate (Class Gastropoda)

Size relative to a 15 cm tall boba cup

Lifespan in the wild:
Around 10 years

Size:
Up to 15 cm long

Weight:
Around 240 g

DANGEROUS ☒
ENDANGERED ☑

SCALY-FOOT SNAIL

SEA PANGOLIN

Just like its common name, the large foot of the scaly-foot snail is distinctively covered with hundreds of overlapping hard dermal scales. This characteristic feature of the snail is similar to the scaly pangolin, which also explains its other nickname, the sea pangolin.

A SCALY DETOX?

Scientists discovered that the scaly-foot snail uses its dermal scales to remove toxic substances! After the symbiotic bacteria in its body produces energy, the waste products become deposited into the snail's scales. This deposition process helps to remove the deadly toxins from the snail's body.

MAGNETO SNAIL!

The scaly-foot snail is the only animal known so far to make a skeleton out of iron! That's right – its shell and dermal scales are coated with a black layer of iron sulphides. Due to its iron-based exterior, this snail has a really tough shell and is attracted to magnets!

A SMALL SNAIL WITH A BIG HEART

Scientists found that the scaly-foot snail has a heart that occupies about 4% of its body volume. A big heart is thought to help the snail transport oxygen more efficiently in an oxygen-poor environment. This snail also has one of the largest hearts relative to body size among other species in the animal kingdom!

NO FEEDING REQUIRED?

With small radula (or tiny teeth) and a reduced gut, the scaly-foot snail feeds very poorly. Instead, the snail gets its nutrients directly from the bacteria stored in a special pouch in its throat. It depends heavily on these bacteria that can convert chemicals from hydrothermal vents into nutrients.

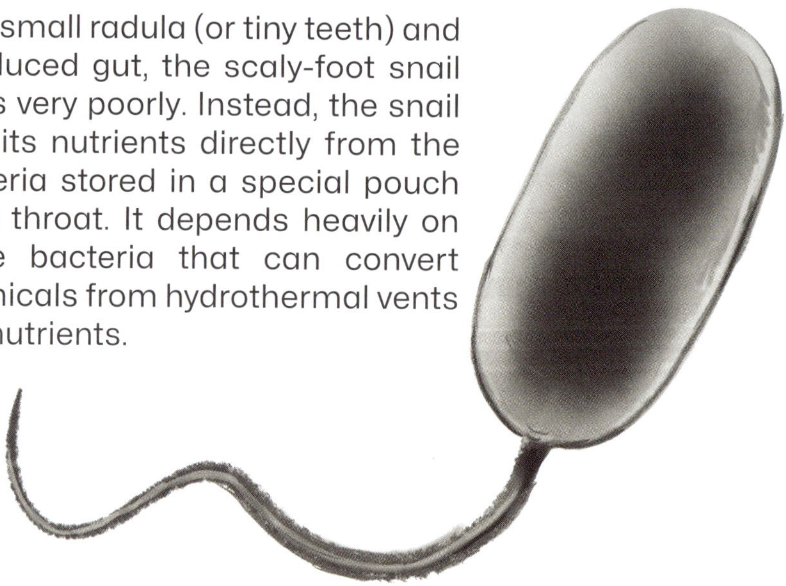

MINED OUT

Deep-sea mining could put the scaly-foot snails in a precarious situation. This species has so far been found in seven locations in the Indian Ocean, six of which are being considered for deep-sea mining. Should mining become allowed, their habitats could be severely reduced or destroyed.

CREATURE REPORT

Common name: Scaly-foot Snail
Species name: *Chrysomallon squamiferum*
Type: Invertebrate (Class Gastropoda)

Size relative to a 15 cm tall boba cup

Lifespan in the wild:
Unknown

Size:
Up to
50 mm long

Weight:
Up to 22 g

DANGEROUS ☒
ENDANGERED ☑

SEA ANGEL

ANGELIC SWIMMERS

Sea angels are beautiful to watch. These translucent sea slugs give off an ethereal illusion as they glide through the sea. They have wing-like appendages (or parapodia), which help them to swim and search for food.

FAMILY KILLERS

When it comes to meal times, sea angels turn into lethal beasts. These carnivorous slugs mostly hunt and eat sea butterflies – their close relatives! Once caught, the sea angels use hooks and their serrated tongue to pull the prey from their shell.

STUCK ONTO YOU

Sea angels can spend up to four hours mating each time! First, they turn their reproductive organs inside out and bind themselves together using specialised suckers. Later, fertilisation takes place as the mating pair sticks together, multi-tasking dancing, swimming and hunting!

NOT ALWAYS NAKED

Baby sea angels are born with shells at first. As they grow older, they undergo metamorphosis, just like a caterpillar changing into a butterfly. Adult sea angels shed their shells to become naked and translucent.

A BITTER TASTE

The sea angel avoids becoming lunch by making its own recipe of bitter-tasting toxins to deter predators! This remarkable feat is the only example where a chemical defence is made by a marine snail and not absorbed from a food source.

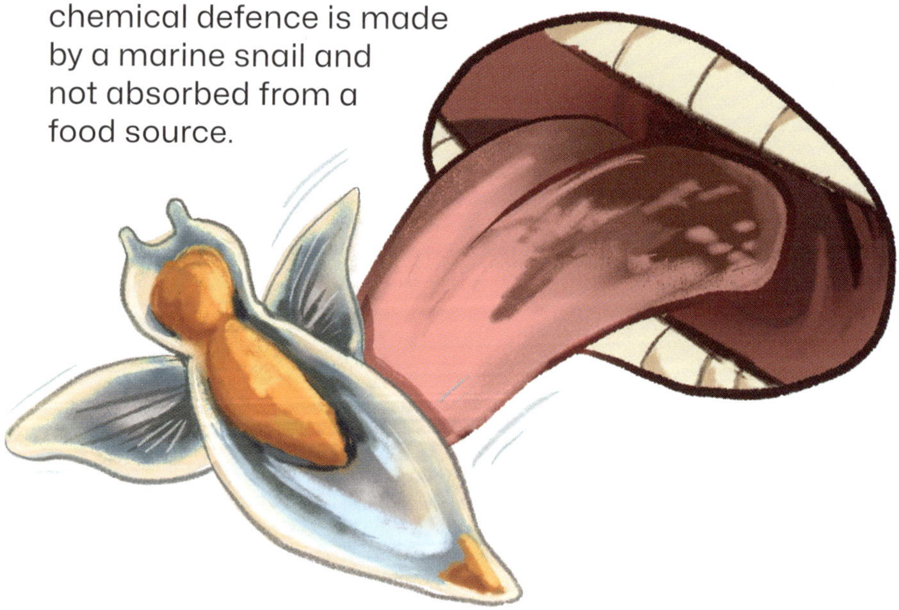

DISSOLVING LUNCH!

As seawater becomes more acidic due to climate change, sea angels could end up with less food in the near future. This is because the increased acidity in seawater can damage the thin shells of their favourite food, the sea butterflies.

CREATURE REPORT

Common name: Sea Angel
Species name: *Clione limacina*
Type: Invertebrate (Class Gastropoda)

Size relative to a 15 cm tall boba cup

Lifespan in the wild:
Unknown

Size:
Up to
5 cm long

Weight:
Unknown

DANGEROUS ☒

ENDANGERED ☒

SUNFLOWER SEA STAR

VORACIOUS SUNFLOWERS

With up to 24 arms, an adult sunflower sea star looks very much like its namesake flower. This northeast Pacific Ocean resident is also the largest sea star with the most arms. This voracious carnivore can move very swiftly when hunting for prey such as the sea urchins, clams and snails.

FRAGMENTED SKELETON

Sea stars have hydrostatic skeletons supporting their shapes by fluid movement. While most sea stars have a single semi-rigid skeleton, the skeleton of a sunflower sea star is disconnected into several parts! The latter allows it to enlarge its mouth much wider for bigger prey.

MOVING HEADS WITHOUT BODIES!

Sea stars have no bodies?! New research found that they lack the genes that dictate a body plan. Sea stars are pretty much head-like creatures that can move and crawl. The sunflower sea star, for instance, can move up to 3 metres per minute on their 15,000 tube feet!

KELP FOREST PROTECTORS

Kelp forests are defenceless against sea urchins, which feed voraciously on kelp seaweed. Luckily, the sunflower sea stars love to eat sea urchins and they indirectly keep the sea urchin numbers in check. Without these sea stars, it could mean the ecological destruction of kelp forests!

SEA STAR WASTING SYNDROME

Around 2013 onwards, a mysterious disease called the sea star wasting syndrome caused the deaths of sea stars from Alaska to Mexico. Diseased sea stars would lose their arms and die within days, leaving behind a gooey mess. The sunflower sea star was one of the most badly affected species.

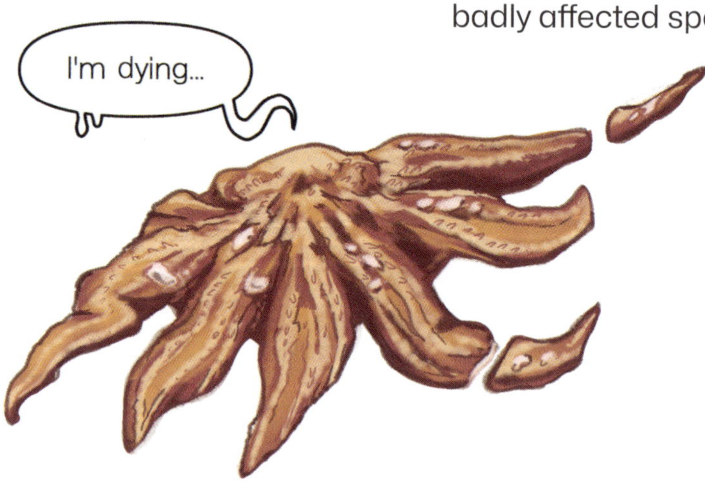

FALLEN STARS

Nearly five billion sunflower sea stars have died since the sea star wasting syndrome outbreak in 2013. This alarming decline prompted conservationists to declare them as critically endangered. Active conservation is underway, while the cause of the disease is being studied.

CREATURE REPORT

Common name: Sunflower Sea Star
Species name: *Pycnopodia helianthoides*
Type: Invertebrate (Class Asteroidea)

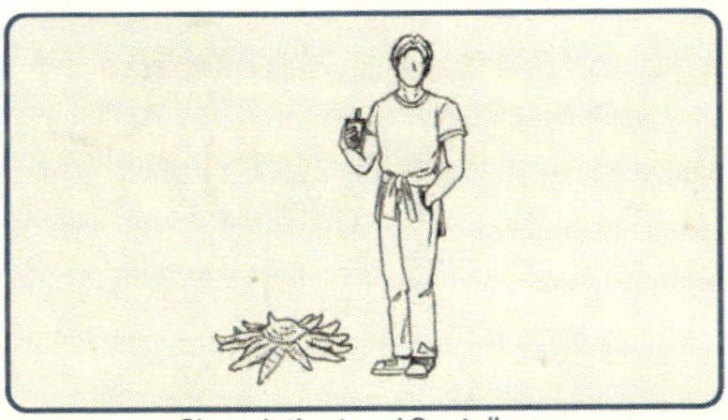

Size relative to a 1.8m tall man

Lifespan in the wild:
20.5 to 65 years

Size:
Around 100 cm, from tip to tip

Weight:
Up to 5 kg

DANGEROUS ☒

ENDANGERED ☑

CROWN-OF-THORNS STARFISH

A PRICKLY HEAP

The thorny crown-of-thorns starfish looks just like the biblical crown of thorns. This large sea star can grow up to 21 arms and its body surface is heavily armoured with prickly spines. These spines are also venomous, which defend them against predators.

THE PAIN MACHINE

Seeing the crown-of-thorns starfish up close can instil a subconscious fear of them! Their hundreds of spines contain a nasty mix of toxins that can cause cellular damage. They can cause extreme pain to any animal (or human!) that come into contact with them.

CORAL EATERS

The crown-of-thorns starfish is a greedy coral-eater! It feeds by pushing its stomach on the corals and releasing digestive enzymes. This process melts the coral tissues into soup! A single adult sea star is said to eat up to 10 m^2 of corals in a year.

HUNGRY SWARMS

When in great numbers, the crown-of-thorns starfish are an absolute menace to coral reefs! Their coral-eating habits can cause significant damage and destruction of reefs. If the sea star outbreaks become more frequent, coral reefs are in grave danger.

STAR(FISH) WARS

Scientists are worried for our corals as the crown-of-thorns starfishes are thriving. Overfishing of reefs could also remove important sea star predators like the giant triton snails. To protect corals, strategic culling of these sea stars can help control their numbers.

REEF PRUNING

All being said, in a balanced coral reef ecosystem, the presence of crown-of-thorns starfish could be a good thing! Their periodic feeding on corals helps maintain coral reef diversity. They can also help to make space for slow-growing corals by eating the fast-growing ones.

CREATURE REPORT

Common name: Crown-of-thorns Starfish
Species name: *Acanthaster planci*
Type: Invertebrate (Class Asteroidea)

Size relative to a 1.8m tall man

Lifespan in the wild:
16 years

Size:
25 to 35 cm
in diameter

Weight:
Up to 3 kg

DANGEROUS ✓

ENDANGERED ✗

YETI CRAB

LOBSTER-LOOKING CRABS

While the yeti crab can look like a lobster, it is actually more closely related to the hermit and coconut crabs. This 10-legged crab has a much smaller fourth pair of walking legs usually hidden from view, which give it an 8-legged appearance.

SMOKING HOT!

Deep-sea hydrothermal vents are like hot springs under the sea. Yeti crabs, which live as deep as 2,000 m, call these seemingly inhospitable habitats their homes. While the vents keep them warm, yeti crabs also avoid getting too close to the hot fluids, for they can become cooked alive!

THE ABOMINABLE SNOW CRAB?

White and fuzzy, the scientists thought the yeti crab looked like the infamous Yeti snowman! *Kiwa hirsuta* was the first yeti crab species discovered in 2005. Its given name, *hirsuta* in Latin, means "hairy" to describe its fuzzy limbs.

I CANNOT SEE WELL

Yeti crabs are born with very poorly developed eyes, making them virtually blind. They use their hairy limbs to navigate the dark seafloor instead. These hairs, called setae, act like tiny sensors to help the crabs in finding food or mates.

FARMING OWN FOOD

When you live on the deep and dark seafloor, food is limited. So, yeti crabs "collect" food by waving their hairy limbs back and forth over hydrothermal vents. This waving behaviour helps them to harvest and farm bacteria from the vents. The crabs would then feed on the nutritious bacteria!

GONE BEFORE YOU KNOW IT?

As humans continue to explore the deep-sea zones, these habitats could become threatened by pollution and utilisation in the future. This could put the benign yeti crabs in danger of losing their homes.

CREATURE REPORT

Common name: Yeti Crab
Species name: *Kiwa hirsuta*
Type: Invertebrate (Class Malacostraca)

Size relative to a 15 cm tall boba cup

Lifespan in the wild:
10 to 20 years

Size:
Around 15 cm long

Weight:
0.9 to 2.3 kg

DANGEROUS ☒
ENDANGERED ?

CLAMKILLER SLIPPER LOBSTER

CRUSTY SLIPPER

Slipper lobsters get their name because of their flattened outer shell which resembles a slipper. Unlike their crab relatives, they have large antennae and no front claws. The clamkiller slipper lobster lives in the deep waters down to 100 m depth around the Indo-West Pacific region.

BEING FLAT IS GOOD

The clamkiller slipper lobster escapes predation by using its flat body! It can lie very flat and still on the sandy bottom, largely unnoticed by predators. The animal can also use its unique colouring as camouflage to blend in with the rocks and seabed.

CLAM KILLER

The clamkiller slipper lobster attacks giant clams (*Tridacna*) and feeds by cracking open the shell with its jaws and legs. For this reason, it has the specific name *tridacnophaga*. This carnivorous animal also feeds on other shellfish, crabs, sea urchins and worms.

BLACK AND WHITE VISION

Slipper lobsters are active at night and need a vision that adapts well to dim light environments. Scientists discovered they have a monochromatic vision that sees the world in different shades of black to white. This helps them to forage efficiently.

TALKING WITH PEE?

Slipper lobsters cannot make their own sounds, so they use pee to communicate! They do so by squirting urine from their faces at the other slipper lobsters. Their urine also contains pheromones, which send chemical signals as messages to convey how they are feeling.

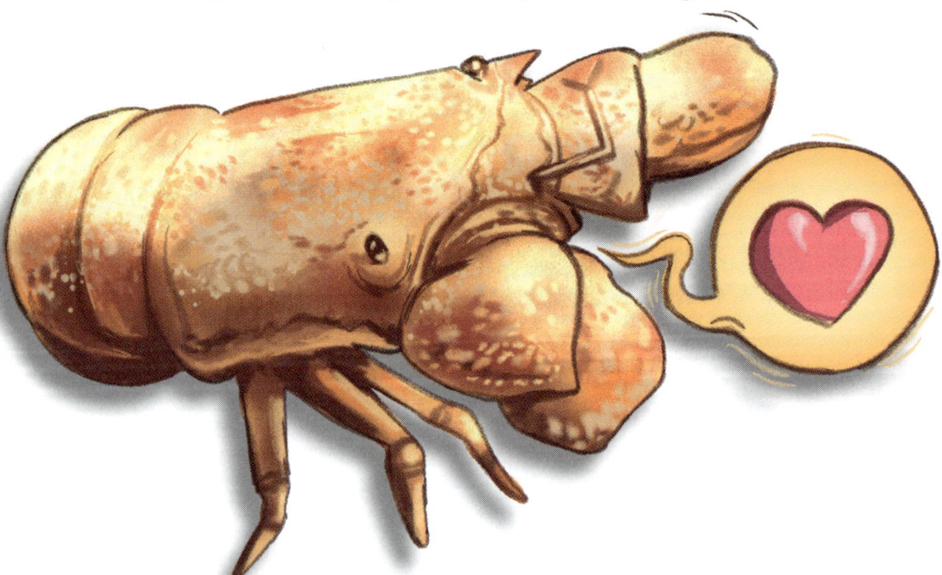

COMMERCIALLY FISHED

These edible slipper lobsters are economically important fisheries. They are heavily fished for their tails, which are popular across the world. Even though their populations are not yet threatened, their numbers may decline due to intensive fishing and climate change.

CREATURE REPORT

Common name: Clamkiller Slipper Lobster
Species name: *Scyllarides tridacnophaga*
Type: Invertebrate (Class Malacostraca)

Size relative to a 15 cm tall boba cup

Lifespan in the wild:
Around 10 to 15 years

Size:
Up to 30 cm long

Weight:
0.5 to 1.5 kg

DANGEROUS	☒
ENDANGERED	☒

NIGHT ANEMONE

HIDDEN IN PLAIN SIGHT

The night anemone is not your usual sea anemone. This species has mastered both camouflage and mimicry! It can change its colour and pattern, and alter its shape. Often, it can appear as corals, seaweeds and even rocks covered with algae.

MASTER OF DISGUISES

To conceal its true form, the night anemone changes its body shape and colour to blend into the surroundings. It hides its real tentacles in the body while only showing its pseudo-tentacles, which can take many forms. This disguise method can both deceive prey and confuse predators!

JACK-IN-THE-BOX

Like the children's toy, the night anemone cranks up to reveal its true body after dark. Its body column extends and stretches upwards, where the mouth and tentacles appear at the top. Pseudo-tentacles surrounding its body column would still remain visible.

FATAL MASQUERADE

Among other sea anemones, the night anemone's venom is said to be one of the most dangerous to humans! In most cases, the sea anemone's toxic venoms can cause severe swelling and irritation to the skin. At worst, the victims may develop acute kidney injury!

POWERED BY SOLAR ENERGY

The night anemone stores microalgae in its tissues. These plant-like cells undergo photosynthesis to produce nutrients for the host anemone.

To maximise light capture, the microalgae are most densely packed in the pseudo-tentacles that extend outwards during the day.

EVADING DETECTION?

Because of their elaborate disguises, the night anemones seemingly avoid attention from predators and humans. Scientists who managed to study them found them challenging to recognise in the field. So, not much is yet known about their populations.

CREATURE REPORT

Common name: Night Anemone
Species name: *Phyllodiscus semoni*
Type: Invertebrate (Class Hexacorallia)

?

Lifespan in the wild: Unknown

Size: Unknown

Weight: Unknown

DANGEROUS ✓

ENDANGERED ?

IMMORTAL JELLYFISH

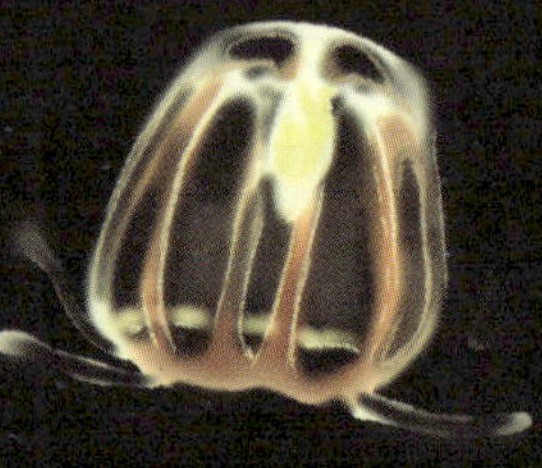

THE YOUTHFUL JELLY

Even though the immortal jellyfish was first described in 1883, its "immortality" was accidentally discovered after a century! When it gets injured or faces stress, such as starvation, the immortal jellyfish prevents its death by shrinking its body size and settling to the seafloor as a blob.

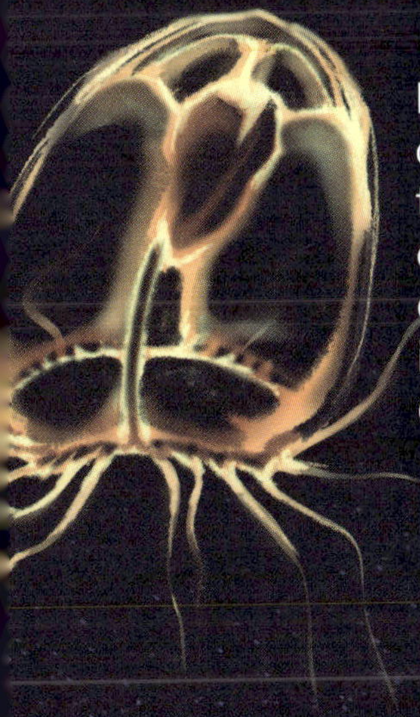

RECYCLING CELLS

It cannot die easily because of a process called transdifferentiation. This means the immortal jellyfish can regularly change its cells to an immature state during times of stress. It can later regrow into a mature jellyfish again! This is an efficient way of cell recycling with potential uses in medicine.

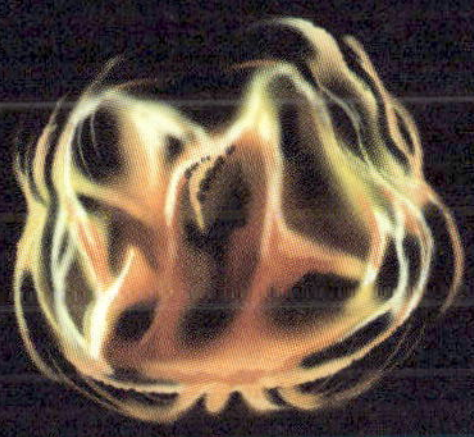

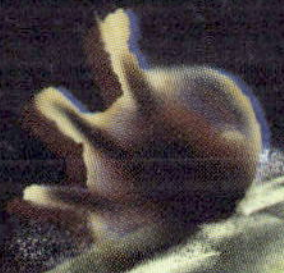

CHAMPION OF REGENERATION

Under the right conditions, a scientist discovered that the immortal jellyfish may regenerate itself up to 10 times over a two year period! Theoretically, this jellyfish can infinitely reverse its life cycle, giving rise to its biological immortality!

WORLD DOMINATION

The cosmopolitan immortal jellyfish is travelling the world's oceans in long-distance ships. The tiny-bodied jellyfish hides in the ballast water that is pumped in and out of vessels to stabilise ships. It is likely to survive the ocean's crossings thanks to its ability to reverse its life cycle when stressed.

DO MY STINGS HURT?

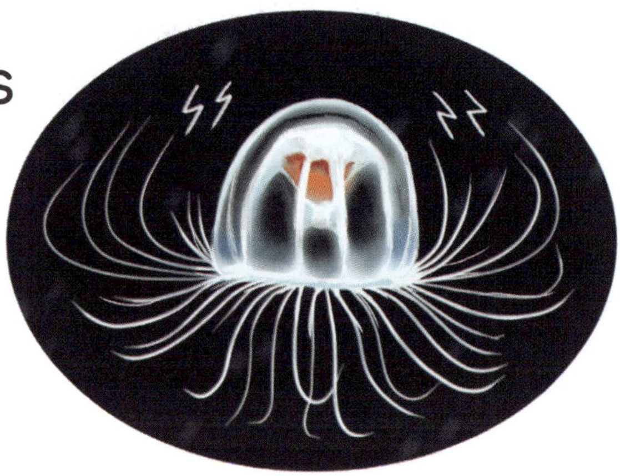

Jellyfish all have tiny stinging cells called cnidocytes in their tentacles. They typically use their stinging cells to paralyse small prey like plankton and fish eggs before eating them. While the immortal jellyfish is not aggressive towards humans, it is still best not to touch it with your bare hands as it can deliver a sting!

CHEATING DEATH?

The immortal jellyfish cannot always cheat death! It can still die from being eaten by fish and sea turtles or when it contracts diseases and injuries. If the jellyfish is in an immature state, starves or gets sick, it cannot reset its life cycle to avoid death.

CREATURE REPORT

Common name: Immortal Jellyfish
Species name: *Turritopsis dohrnii*
Type: Invertebrate (Class Hydrozoa)

Size relative to a 15 cm tall boba cup

Lifespan in the wild:
Unknown

Size:
4.5 to 12.0 mm long

Weight:
<1 g

DANGEROUS ?

ENDANGERED ?

GLOSSARY

Aggressive is the state of being ready or likely to attack or confront a potential opponent.

Acidity is the state of being acidic or describes the amount of acid present in a substance.

Basking, sometimes known as sunbathing, is a behaviour used by animals to help raise and regulate their body temperatures, reduce the energy needed for temperature maintenance or provide comfort.

Blubber refers to the fatty tissues of marine mammals, such as whales and seals.

Bioluminescence is the production and emission of light by living organisms through chemical reactions in their bodies.

Body plan refers to the basic structure of the organs and tissues within an organism's body. In the animal kingdom, there are two major themes in body plans: symmetry and the organisation of tissues and body cavities.

Breaching refers to an animal (such as a whale) rising and breaking through the surface of the water.

Bycatch are animals that fishermen sometimes catch and discard because they do not want, cannot sell or are not allowed to keep. Bycatch can be fish but also includes other animals, such as dolphins, whales, sea turtles and seabirds, which become hooked or entangled in fishing gear.

Camouflage is when animals blend in with their surroundings so they cannot be seen by other living things.

Cephalopods are a class of invertebrates that includes animals without a backbone, such as the octopus, squid, cuttlefish and nautilus.

Climate change describes a change in the average conditions – such as high and low temperatures and amount of rainfall – in a region over a long period of time.

Cosmopolitan is used to describe a plant or animal found worldwide.

Curio is an object or article valued because it is strange or rare.

Dermal denticles are tooth-like or plate-like scales that cover the skin of sharks and rays.

A **dialect** is a form of a language spoken by a group of people. For example, people who live in the same place share a dialect.

Docile describes the peaceful and quiet nature of animals. They are also not usually aggressive.

Electrocution describes the injury or killing of someone by electric shock.

Elusive means hard to find or catch.

Endemic species describes a species of animal or plant that is found only in a specific location and found naturally nowhere else.

Enzyme is a substance made by cells of plants and animals that speed up chemical reactions.

Fatal describes something that can cause or is capable of causing death.

Fishery is the business of catching, packing or selling fish and other seafood.

Immortality is the idea of something staying alive or lasting forever.

Masquerade means to pretend to be someone or something else.

Metabolism is a group of chemical reactions that keep living things alive.

Metamorphosis is a dramatic process some animals go through to reach adulthood.

Mimicry is when one organism copies, imitates or resembles a different organism.

A **mollusc** is an animal with a soft body, such as a snail, clam or octopus.

Monochrome refers to things with tones or shades of only one colour.

Nutrients are basic units of energy sources for all animals. Some examples include carbohydrates, lipids, nucleic acids, proteins, minerals and vitamins.

Paralysis refers to losing the ability to move in part or most of the body, typically due to illness, poison or injury.

A **parasite** is an organism that gets nutrients by living on or in an organism of another species.

A **pheromone** is a chemical substance made by an animal, which serves as a signal to other individuals of the same species to take part in activities such as mating and feeding.

Photophore is a light-producing organ found in some organisms.

Photosynthesis is when plants, algae and certain bacteria use sunlight to make food.

Pollution happens when the environment is exposed to, or dirtied, by waste, chemicals and other harmful substances.

Pseudo means something is not genuine or fake.

The **radula** is a toothed ribbon-like organ in molluscs used for scraping food and bringing it into the mouth.

Regeneration refers to how organisms replace lost or damaged parts by growing them again.

Seagrass is a marine flowering plant that lives in or close to the sea.

Toxins are substances made by plants and animals that are poisonous to humans.

Unpalatable means unappetising, inedible or distasteful.

Unregulated describes a business or activity not controlled and directed by rules or laws.

Voracious means craving or eating large quantities of food.

Venom is a toxic substance made by some animals that is poisonous to humans and animals.

Vocalisation is a sound produced with the voice or the act of making sounds with the voice.

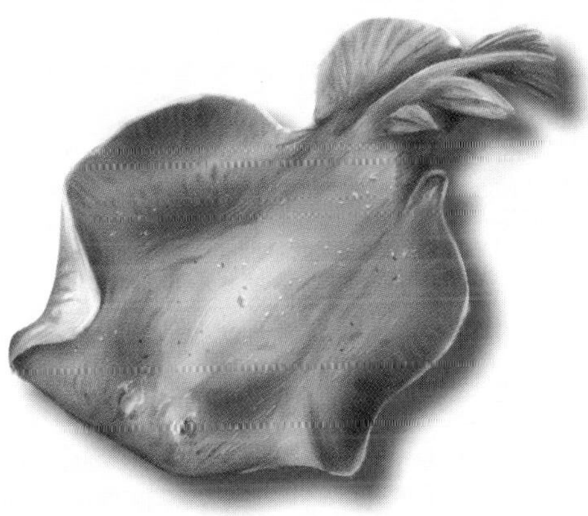

ACKNOWLEDGEMENTS

First of all, I would like to say a big thank you to whoever is holding this book right now! We are very grateful for your kind support of our book.

To all the expert reviewers who answered my call for help in fact-checking the species' information, I am most thankful for your time in sharing your candid feedback to ensure the accuracy of the content. Thank you to Louisa Ponnampalam, Olga Filatova, Rushan bin Abdul Rahman, Sankar Ananthanarayanan, Naomi Clark-Shen, Kent Elson S. Sorgon, Adam Lim, Tan Koh Siang, Teresa S. Tay, Lee Li Keat, Chen Chong, Choo Le Qin, Jose Christopher E. Mendoza, Nicholas Yap and Ling Min Kang.

To my family, I am grateful to my partner and best friend, Alex, for being my biggest critic and supporter throughout the years together. And to my dearest children, Ada, Maya and Remus, for inspiring me daily to keep doing good for our oceans.

A 2021 Pew Fellowship in Marine Conservation awarded to the author generously supported the development of this book.

ABOUT THE AUTHOR

Dr. Neo Mei Lin is a marine biologist, science communicator, environmental advocate and a mother of three. Born and raised in urban Singapore, she spent most of her childhood exploring nature areas with her family. These experiences led her to develop a strong curiosity about nature and its workings. She believes in using her voice to amplify important environmental conservation messages that people need to hear. She is also the author of *A Field Guide to Giant Clams of the Indo-Pacific*, which features her favourite marine animal, the giant clam!

ABOUT THE ILLUSTRATOR

Adel is an illustrator with a mechanical engineering degree and a love for all things wildlife. Her art is a blend of international art influences, including the fantastical creatures captured with a rough painterly style and bold colours. She also works as a muralist and spray paints in her free time. Her main subjects are wildlife or creature designs with a touch of psychedelic as she tries to capture the already strange world in an even stranger way. Check out her illustrations on Instagram @sykonebabblin!